D1521119

Teen Privacy Rights

Other titles in the *Hot Issues* series

Cult Awareness
A Hot Issue
ISBN 0-7660-1196-8

Cyberdanger and
Internet Safety
A Hot Issue
ISBN 0-7660-1368-5

Date Rape
A Hot Issue
ISBN 0-7660-1198-4

Drug Abuse
and Teens
A Hot Issue
ISBN 0-7660-1372-3

Eating Disorders
A Hot Issue
ISBN 0-7660-1336-7

Endangered Animals
of North America
A Hot Issue
ISBN 0-7660-1373-1

Hate and Racist
Groups
A Hot Issue
ISBN 0-7660-1371-5

Multiethnic Teens
and Cultural Identity
A Hot Issue
ISBN 0-7660-1201-8

Sexually
Transmitted Diseases
A Hot Issue
ISBN 0-7660-1192-5

Stalking
A Hot Issue
ISBN 0-7660-1364-2

Teens,
Depression,
and the Blues
A Hot Issue
ISBN 0-7660-1369-3

Teens and
Pregnancy
A Hot Issue
ISBN 0-7660-1365-0

Teen Smoking
and Tobacco Use
A Hot Issue
ISBN 0-7660-1359-6

The Women's
Movement
and Young Women
Today
A Hot Issue
ISBN 0-7660-1200-X

Teen Privacy Rights

A Hot Issue

Deanne Durrett

HOT
ISSUES

Enslow Publishers, Inc.

40 Industrial Road	PO Box 38
Box 398	Aldershot
Berkeley Heights, NJ 07922	Hants GU12 6BP
USA	UK

Library of Congress Cataloging-in-Publication Data

Durrett, Deanne, 1940–
Teen privacy rights : a hot issue / Deanne Durrett.
      p. cm. — (Hot issues)
Includes bibliographical references and index. Summary: Examines all
aspects of teen privacy rights, from the history of this topic to how it
came to be an issue. Also discusses the importance of knowing and
exercising your rights.
ISBN 0-7660-1374-X (hard)

1. Teenagers—Legal status, laws, etc.—United States—Juvenile
literature. 2. Privacy, Right of—United States—Juvenile literature.
[1. Teenagers—Legal status, laws, etc. 2. Privacy, Right of.] I. Title.
II. Series.

KF479.Z9 D87   2000
346.7301'35—dc2l
    00-008413

Printed in the United States of America

10 9 8 7 6 5 4 3 2 1

To Our Readers:
All Internet addresses in this book were active and appropriate when we
went to press. Any comments or suggestions can be sent by e-mail to
Comments@enslow.com or to the address on the back cover.

Illustration Credits: AP Wide World Photos, pp. 3, 12, 15, 25, 38,
54; Corel Corporation, p. 29; Skjold Photographs, pp. 9, 42, 44, 49.

Cover Illustration: AP Wide World Photos

Contents

Chapter 1

How Privacy Became an Issue

On March 7, 1980, two New Jersey high-school freshmen slipped into a rest room to smoke cigarettes. The girls knew smoking in the rest room was against school rules. They did not expect to get caught, but they were. The teacher who caught the girls smoking marched them down the hall to face Vice Principal Theodore Choplick. Upon questioning, one girl admitted she had been smoking. The other, however, denied that she had been smoking. She also insisted that she did not smoke at all.

Based on the teacher's eyewitness account, Choplick suspected that the fourteen-year-old was lying. He took her into his office and asked to look in her purse. When he opened her purse, he found a pack of cigarettes. Removal of the cigarettes uncovered some cigarette rolling papers. Knowing rolling papers are often used with marijuana, Choplick searched the purse further. He found a small amount of marijuana, a pipe, and some empty plastic bags. He also found a large amount of money in one-dollar bills. There was a list of students who owed the girl money and two letters that indicated she was selling marijuana.

Choplick gave the evidence to the local police. They filed charges. In the court proceedings that followed, the search and the student's right to privacy became an issue. After a series of appeals, the case was heard by the U.S. Supreme Court.[1] The *New Jersey* v. *T.L.O.* decision became the legal standard (or guide) for school searches. This included when and how school officials could conduct searches without violating students' privacy rights.

Teachers Acting in Place of Parents

Students' privacy rights became a Supreme Court issue in the 1980s. There was a time, however, when most people gave little thought to the legal aspects of privacy. Privacy concerns of minors (children under the age of eighteen) were a family matter. Family privacy usually involved closed doors, pulled window blinds, and lowered voices. Minors' privacy might have included secret hiding places for diaries and private notes and letters. People who secretly listened in on minors' telephone conversations may have posed a threat. Still, siblings were the most common invaders of minors' privacy.

Parents (the authorities within the home) had the right to search whatever needed searching in the name of caring for and training their children. At that time, teachers and principals (the authorities at school) were legally considered *in loco parentis* (Latin for "in the place of a parent"). This means they were acting in the role of parents while children were at school.[2] Thus, the Fourth Amendment

*A*t one time, teachers were legally considered *in loco parentis* while children were at school. This means that teachers were acting the role of parents in the classroom.

did not apply at school. (The Fourth Amendment protects people from unlawful search and seizure by government officials.) Teachers and principals could conduct searches to enforce the rules. They were expected to use good judgment, much the same as a parent would at home. Most offenses involved cigarette smoking, cheating on exams, or petty theft. Discipline was handled within the school. And most parents were comfortable giving school officials this authority.

Times changed, however. Drugs and guns arrived on school campuses. In many areas, the threat of criminal activity changed school grounds from safe areas to danger zones. School officials sometimes became involved in law enforcement.

What Changed?

In the last half of the twentieth century, the United States experienced many changes. The population rapidly increased. Many families moved from rural areas to urban areas (cities). Urban schools became crowded. The cost of living rose and mothers joined their husbands in the workforce. This left many children on their own before and after school.

During this time, the drug culture that had invaded college campuses in the 1960s slowly crept into high schools. It soon spread to lower and lower grades. Movies and television programs became more violent. More powerful guns became available to the general public, and easier for minors to obtain.[3]

Violence followed drugs to America's schools. Major discipline problems erupted in middle and high schools across the nation. The U.S. Department of Education reports that from 1997 to 1999, nearly four thousand students were expelled from public schools for bringing guns on campus.[4]

A gun on campus is a serious concern. It can be used to kill or injure several people in a few seconds. Most guns can be hidden easily and can remain undetected until used. This dangerous situation adds crime detection to the teacher's duties, which many people consider to be an unfair

JUVENILE COURT

Most cases against juveniles are heard by a judge in juvenile court. There is no jury and no one is allowed in the courtroom who does not need to be there. Those allowed in the courtroom include the judge, lawyers, court officials, the juvenile, and his or her parents or guardians. If witnesses are called, they are only in the courtroom long enough to give their testimony. Members of the press arc not allowed in the courtroom.

When crimes involving a juvenile are reported in the media, the identity of the juvenile is usually withheld. In the past, all juvenile court records were sealed. However, a case that reaches the U.S. Supreme Court is used in deciding other cases and becomes public record. Therefore, juvenile defendants are listed in court records by their initials. This is done to protect their privacy. Thus, the student at Piscataway High School became known as T.L.O.

burden. It also brings school safety and student privacy rights into direct conflict.

Safety v. Privacy

Most parents demand safety for their children during school hours. Many parents are more concerned about security than privacy rights. Some, however, have filed lawsuits charging school officials with violations of privacy rights. Most of these suits resulted from searches that produced evidence that a student was involved in criminal activity. In the

*W*hen there is a threat of danger, most parents are more concerned with students' safety than with their privacy rights. Here, a student's backpack is searched by a volunteer after graffiti that warned of student killings was found in a school bathroom.

New Jersey v. *T.L.O.* decision, the U.S. Supreme Court tried to clarify earlier rulings dealing with school searches. In these rulings the courts recognized teachers and school officials as employees of the state. Thus, a school search conducted without probable cause violated the student's Fourth Amendment rights. The Court also realized that the duty to protect students from harm sometimes requires immediate action—such as a search. In writing the majority opinion, Justice Byron White tried to balance students' rights with the schools' responsibilities. (A majority opinion is a paper written to explain how the Justices who voted in favor of a ruling reached their decision.) White wrote, "Students in public schools are protected by the Fourth Amendment. At the same time, a balance must be struck between the student's legitimate expectation of privacy and the school's need to maintain an environment of learning."[5]

The *T.L.O.* decision placed school officials in a unique position. School officials are responsible for supervising and protecting minors much as a parent would do. At the same time, these government employees may face charges if they violate a student's privacy rights. The Court did not provide clear guidelines for ensuring students' safety while protecting their privacy rights.

Chapter 2

The Reasons for Privacy

The concept of privacy includes the rights and responsibilities that govern how personal information can be collected and revealed. It includes the power to control what other people can know about you, the right to keep certain aspects of your life to yourself, and the right to be alone at times. Privacy also includes the right to keep personal belongings for one's own use.

When Justice Louis Brandeis took his seat on the Supreme Court in 1916, he believed that the United States Constitution had established a right to privacy. He believed that this precious right barred the government from invading private lives. He defined privacy as "the right to be let alone—the most comprehensive [broad] of rights and the right most valued by civilized men."[1] In later years, however, new privacy issues arose.

Privacy was an important aspect of women's rights issues in the 1970s. In the 1973 *Roe* v. *Wade* decision, the U.S. Supreme Court broadened privacy rights. The Court ruled that abortion (removing an embryo or fetus from the womb to end a pregnancy)

*T*he debate over the 1973 *Roe* v. *Wade* decision still rages on. Here, demonstrators on both sides of the issue attend a rally to mark the twenty-seventh anniversary of the U.S. Supreme Court's decision to legalize abortion.

in the first three months of pregnancy is a private matter. Privacy became a student issue in the 1980s. The Court gave limited privacy rights to students in the 1985 *New Jersey* v. *T.L.O.* decision. In the 1990s, the privacy issue was hurled into cyberspace. Huge computer databases and high-speed searches had made almost everyone's personal information easily available. And almost anyone could get the information. No one knew how this information might be used—or how much harm could be done with it. As a result, federal legislators began to consider steps to protect privacy in the computer age.

Constitutional Right to Privacy

The word *privacy* is not used in the United States Constitution. Neither is it mentioned in the Bill of

Rights or in any of the additional amendments. Three of the ten amendments in the Bill of Rights, however, did deal with the privacy concerns of Americans in the 1700s.

The writers of the Constitution wanted to protect the privacy of the American people from the government. They took this step because, while the colonies were under British rule, the British government had shown no respect for the colonists' personal privacy. For example, the 1765 Quartering Act forced the colonists to provide lodging and supplies for British soldiers living in America.[2] The original act called for housing British troops in the colonies' public and commercial buildings. On June 2, 1775, the British amended the act to include housing British soldiers in private homes.[3] The colonists endured other unjust practices under British rule. These included unfair taxes and unreasonable search and seizure. These practices finally enraged the colonists and led to revolt.

The Third Amendment

After the Revolutionary War, the colonies became an independent country, the United States of America. The Founding Fathers established a strong government when they ratified the United States Constitution. One of the signers, Patrick Henry, recognized the strength of the new government. He alerted his fellow patriots to a possible danger. He said, "Here we may have troops in time of peace. They may be billeted [assigned lodging] in any manner—to tyrannize, oppress, and crush us."[4] In other words, Henry was concerned about where the new government would house its soldiers. He saw the need to protect the American home from this invasion as greater "than ever it was in any government before."[5] With this in mind, the framers (writers) of the Constitution wrote the Third Amendment, which states:

> No soldier shall, in time of peace, be quartered in any house without the consent of the owner; nor in time of war, but in the manner prescribed by law.[6]

The Third Amendment has served the American people well. In fact, the thought of quartering troops on private property against the owner's will now seems absurd. Today, the Supreme Court translates the Third Amendment to guarantee the privacy of a person's home. It recognizes the home as a place of refuge and security. Others may not enter it without permission. Government officials may enter without permission only if they have cause. This means they must have a good reason. Such reasons include a concern that someone inside is injured or dead.

The Fourth Amendment

The framers of the Constitution also wanted to prevent other types of oppression the colonists had suffered under British rule. One of these was unreasonable search and seizure. The British Parliament issued writs of assistance (blanket search warrants) to their law enforcement and military officials in the colonies. These documents were universal and perpetual. *Universal* means they could be used to search anyone. *Perpetual* means they would not expire. Armed with a writ of assistance, the bearer could search any person or place at any time. In fact, customs officials and British military personnel used the writs to break into colonists' homes. In February 1761, attorney James Otis delivered a lengthy

Unreasonable Search and Seizure

Before the American colonies declared their independence, they were governed by Great Britain. Under British rule, government officials could search any colonist, the colonist's home, or the colonist's property for any reason. They could also take or use (seize) anything that belonged to the colonist. The colonists considered this unreasonable. The Fourth Amendment to the U.S. Constitution was written to protect against unreasonable search and seizure.

speech against the writs of assistance before the superior court in Boston. He stated, "A man's house is his castle; and while he is quiet, he is as well guarded as a prince in his castle."[7] Upholding this principle, the Founding Fathers wrote the Fourth Amendment. With these words, they added protection against unreasonable search and seizure:

> The right of the people to be secure in their persons, houses, papers, and effects, against unreasonable searches and seizures, shall not be violated, and no warrants shall issue, but upon probable cause, supported by oath or affirmation, and particularly describing the place to be searched, and the persons or things to be seized.[8]

The Fourth Amendment also protects people who are suspected of committing a crime. It forbids government officials and law enforcement agents from searching anyone without probable cause. They must have reason to believe that the person has committed a crime. This protection extends to the person's belongings. It may include purses, pockets, backpacks, cars, boats, personal papers, and computers in homes.

The Fifth Amendment

The Fifth Amendment protects the rights of people who are accused of a crime. It protects those who might be questioned in an investigation. It also protects people who might be called as witnesses in a trial. Any person may refuse to answer any question that may be asked by a law enforcement agent or in court. The person can refuse to answer on the grounds that the information could be used against him or her in court. Refusing to answer a possibly damaging question is known as "taking the Fifth," or claiming Fifth Amendment rights. The Supreme Court has decided that anyone placed under arrest must be made aware of their Fifth Amendment rights. The *Miranda* v. *Arizona* (1966) Supreme Court ruling states:

> An individual held for interrogation [questioning] must be clearly informed that he has the right to consult with a lawyer and have the lawyer with him during interrogation . . . [that he has] the right to remain silent and that anything stated can be used in evidence against him.[9]

As a result of this Supreme Court ruling, Ernesto Miranda, a confessed criminal, was set free. His Fifth Amendment rights had not been made clear to him. He claimed that he did not know he had the right to remain silent before he confessed to a crime. Since then, the law requires the reading of the *Miranda rights* when someone is placed under arrest. These rights include being told, "You have the right to

Miranda Rights

1. You have the right to remain silent.

2. Anything you say can and will be used against you in a court of law.

3. If you are under the age of 18, anything you say can be used against you in a juvenile court prosecution for a juvenile offense and can also be used against you in an adult court criminal prosecution if the juvenile court decides that you are to be tried as an adult.

4. You have the right to talk to an attorney before answering any questions.

5. You have the right to have your attorney present during the questioning.

6. If you cannot afford an attorney, one will be appointed for you without cost, before or during questioning, if you desire.

7. Do you understand these rights?

I have read or have had read to me the above explanation of my constitutional rights and I understand those rights.

_____   _____
                                               Suspect's signature

Understanding my constitutional rights I have decided not to exercise these rights at this time. Any statements made by me are made freely, voluntarily, and without threats or promises of any kind.

_____   _____
Officer's signature   Suspect's signature

_____   _____
Date/time   Location

remain silent. Anything you say can and will be used against you in a court of law."[10]

Privacy Rights Today

Privacy rights today are defined through a patch-work of Supreme Court decisions. These decisions are based on understanding the intent of the authors of the Constitution when they wrote the document more than two hundred years ago. That understanding must then be applied to the case before the Court in modern times.

As drugs and violence have invaded America's schools, a new controversy has arisen. It involves the privacy rights of students. One student, T.L.O., took this issue all the way to the U.S. Supreme Court. In appealing a lower court decision, she asked that the evidence found in her purse be excluded. She claimed that the evidence had been illegally obtained. The vice principal had violated her right to privacy when he searched her purse.

Chapter 3

Student Rights Go to Court

Before 1969, few people thought about students' rights. Students studied the Constitution, but it wasn't clear exactly how the Constitution applied to them. The Supreme Court first addressed the issue of students' constitutional rights in the 1969 *Tinker* v. *Des Moines* decision.

The case was filed on behalf of Mary Beth and John F. Tinker. The thirteen- and fifteen-year-old siblings took part in a 1965 nationwide protest of the Vietnam War. As part of the protest, they wore black armbands to school. This was against school policy. As a result, Mary and John were suspended from school. They argued that students have First Amendment rights. In their view, the school's policy violated these rights. It denied them freedom of speech. The Supreme Court agreed. The decision included a statement that would be used in future cases involving students' rights. It said: "It can hardly be argued that either students or teachers shed their constitutional rights to freedom of speech or expression at the schoolhouse gate."[1]

Six years later, *Goss* v. *Lopez* brought before the Supreme Court a student's right to due process. *Due process* means that certain rules, set by the government, must be followed in all legal proceedings. The right to due process is guaranteed by the Fourteenth Amendment.

In the 1975 case, Dwight Lopez and several other students were suspended from school after a destructive lunchroom disturbance. They were not given an opportunity to tell their version of the incident. Some of them had not participated in the disturbance. These students felt their right to due process had been violated. Lopez and the other students filed a class action suit against the school. Lopez later testified that "at least 75 other students were suspended from his school on the same day . . . [and] he was . . . an innocent bystander."[2] He

Probable Cause

*P*robable cause is a reason to believe a specific person is or has been involved in a specific crime. Law enforcement officials must also believe that evidence of the crime will be found during a search. Unless a suspect is caught in the act of committing a crime, a search warrant is required for a search. Search warrants are obtained from judges. Before issuing a search warrant, the judge must be convinced that the searchers will probably find evidence of a crime.

claimed that he did not have a chance to say he was innocent.

The Court ruled that the students did have a right to due process. The decision stated that a student facing suspension should be given notice. He or she has a right to a hearing. At the hearing, the student should be "told what he is accused of doing and what the basis of the accusation is . . . [and should be] given an opportunity to explain his version of the facts."[3] The hearing should be held before the student is suspended. Some students, however, may pose an immediate threat to other students or property. In such cases, the hearing can be held after the student has been removed from school. The suspension would then be lifted if the student is proved innocent.

These landmark decisions dealing with freedom of speech and due process determined that students do have constitutional rights. They laid the foundation for other court rulings on students' rights. For example, the *Tinker* v. *Des Moines* decision considered the teacher/student relationship. The Court ruled that teachers and other school authorities are more like state officials than parent substitutes. This created a need for further evaluation of students' rights and Fourth Amendment protection against illegal search and seizure.

T.L.O.

New Jersey v. *T.L.O.* involved Vice Principal Theodore Choplick and a junior at Piscataway High School in New Jersey. Choplick had years of experience as vice principal. He had routinely searched suspected wrongdoers' purses, wallets, and book bags. He "investigated whatever needed investigating" to maintain discipline. He saw himself as a stand-in parent. He said, "We are responsible for them. I treat them like they are my children."[4] Choplick had no idea that anyone would question this long-standing school policy. He was surprised that the search of a student's purse would result in a court case. He had never dreamed that such a case would be argued in three state courts and become a U.S. Supreme Court landmark decision.

When Choplick searched T.L.O.'s purse on March 7, 1980, he expected to find evidence that she had broken school rules. He found evidence, however, that T.L.O. had also broken the law. Following school policy, Choplick called the girl's mother and

*S*chools search lockers or student property for drugs, guns, or when a specific act of violence is threatened. Here, a police dog inspects student backpacks for drugs.

the police. He turned the evidence over to the police. A short while later, the mother escorted her daughter to the police station. The police informed T.L.O. of her Miranda rights. They then questioned her about the evidence found in her purse. At first, T.L.O. claimed she was innocent. Then she confessed to selling marijuana at school. She admitted that she had sold between fifteen and twenty marijuana cigarettes that day. As punishment for breaking school rules, T.L.O. received a three-day suspension. She received an additional seven-day suspension for possession of marijuana on campus.[5]

Since selling marijuana is a violation of the law, charges were filed in the Juvenile and Domestic Relations Court of Middlesex County. Based on the evidence found during the search and her confession, T.L.O. was charged with "possession of marijuana with the intent to distribute."[6] This means she had it and she planned to sell it.

Her parents believed T.L.O.'s Fourth Amendment rights had been violated. They hired a lawyer to fight the charges in juvenile court. The lawyer argued that the vice principal did not have probable cause to search T.L.O's purse for marijuana. The search, then, violated T.L.O's Fourth Amendment rights. The lawyer moved to suppress the evidence. According to the exclusionary rule, evidence that is obtained in searches that violate Fourth Amendment rights cannot be used in court. The lawyer wanted the evidence thrown out of court. Without the evidence found in T.L.O.'s purse, no one would have known that T.L.O. had been involved in drug dealing. There would have been no grounds for the charges.

This would have been a solid argument except that the incident happened at school. The search

The Exclusionary Rule

The U.S. Supreme Court decided there should be some penalty in the event that law enforcement agents conduct searches without probable cause. The Court did this to protect the Fourth Amendment rights of people who are suspected of committing a crime. It ruled that evidence obtained during an illegal search cannot be used in court. In other words, the evidence is excluded from the trial. The exclusionary rule is not part of the Fourth Amendment. It is sometimes a matter of controversy, because criminals are sometimes released when evidence that would prove their guilt cannot be used.

was conducted by a school official on school property. The Juvenile and Domestic Relations Court denied the motion to suppress the evidence, stating:

> A school official may properly conduct a search of a student's person if the official has a reasonable suspicion that a crime has been or is in the process of being committed, or reasonable cause to believe that the search is necessary to maintain school discipline or enforce school policies.[7]

Reasonable suspicion requires less evidence than probable cause. Thus, the court decided that the vice principal acted properly in his decision to search T.L.O.'s purse. On January 8, 1982, T.L.O. was found to be delinquent. She was sentenced to one year's probation.

T.L.O. appealed this decision. The appellate division court (court of appeals) agreed that there had been no violation of the Fourth Amendment. The court raised an additional question: Did T.L.O. knowingly and voluntarily give up her Fifth Amendment rights before she confessed?

T.L.O. then brought the case before the Supreme Court of New Jersey. The state supreme court overturned the decision of the lower courts. It ordered the suppression of the evidence, stating, "If an official search violates constitutional rights, the evidence is not admissible in criminal proceedings." From the state court the case went to the U.S. Supreme Court.

The state of New Jersey did not want to pursue T.L.O. further. It brought the case before the U.S. Supreme Court so that the Constitution could be clarified. It wanted the Court to examine the privacy of schoolchildren and the responsibility of school officials. The attorney for the state of New Jersey asked the Court for a ruling that would help balance students' rights with the school's responsibility to maintain a safe campus.

Supreme Court

The Supreme Court had recognized the unique privacy rights and safety concerns present on school campuses. The Court had not ruled, however, on how to balance the two. School officials were caught in a dilemma. Searches were sometimes necessary to keep students safe on campus. Yet a search could result in a violation of student privacy rights. With no Supreme Court decision for reference, lower courts faced with similar suits delivered varying decisions. Some held that school officials

*T*he U.S. Supreme Court has yet to rule decisively on how to balance safety concerns with student privacy rights on school campuses.

represented the government. They had to have probable cause for searches. This meant they had to obtain a search warrant unless there was an immediate danger. Other courts considered school officials to be *in loco parentis*. This meant they were not bound by the Fourth Amendment. They could search students and their belongings just as a parent could. Still others held that the Fourth Amendment applied to students in a limited way. In their view, only reasonable suspicion, not probable cause, was necessary for a search.

Landmark Decision

In examining T.L.O.'s case, the nine Supreme Court justices agreed that schoolchildren have "legitimate expectations of privacy." This means that students should be able to have a certain amount of privacy on campus. The justices agreed that school is a unique situation. School officials must respect the students' constitutional right to privacy. At the same time, they must maintain discipline and a safe learning environment. In striking a balance, the Court slightly limited students' Fourth Amendments rights. The Court also created these guidelines for school searches:

> Under ordinary circumstances, a search of a student by a teacher or other school official will be "justified at its inception" [legal from the beginning] when there are reasonable grounds for suspecting that the search will turn up evidence that the student has violated or is violating either the law or the rules of the school. Such a search will be permissible in its scope when the measures adopted are reasonably related to the objectives of the search and not

excessively intrusive in light of the age and sex of the student and nature of the infraction.[8]

New Jersey v. *T.L.O.* became the landmark case providing legal authority for all cases involving students' Fourth Amendment rights.

The Court intended that the T.L.O. decision would establish that students have Fourth Amendment rights. At the same time, it would provide a basic standard for school searches. This standard would be used by the lower courts. They would keep students' privacy rights and the school's responsibility to maintain a safe learning environment in balance.

As the highest federal court, the U.S. Supreme Court is responsible for interpreting the Constitution. It must make sure that state and federal laws do not infringe on Constitutional rights. Whether students have Fourth Amendment rights is a constitutional matter. This was properly decided by the Supreme Court. The nation's schools, however, are operated by state governments. Therefore, states have set their own legal guidelines for school searches. These guidelines may vary from state to state. However, they all must follow within the U.S. Supreme Court ruling. Within the states, school districts have set their own policies governing student searches. These must, in turn, follow state laws.

Unresolved Questions

As the U.S. Supreme Court expected, many cases involving students' privacy rights followed the *T.L.O.* decision. This decision addressed one specific case. It involved only the search of a student's purse, which is personal property. It did not address whether a student has a "legitimate expectation of privacy" in lockers, desks, or other areas that the school provides for the storage of the students' school supplies. Furthermore, the *T.L.O.* decision did not consider the use of drug-sniffing dogs. It did not determine whether reasonable suspicion must target a particular individual, or whether probable cause is required once school authorities request police assistance in a search.

Chapter 4

Resolving the Unanswered Questions

In the *T.L.O.* case, the U.S. Supreme Court decided that the Fourth Amendment applies to students. The decision states:

> Schoolchildren have legitimate expectations of privacy. They may find it necessary to carry with them a variety of legitimate, noncontraband [legal] items, and there is no reason to conclude that they have necessarily waived all rights to privacy in such items by bringing them onto school grounds.[1]

This means that the Court recognized that students must carry certain personal items to school. These might include keys, money, personal hygiene and grooming items, wallets, purses, photographs, letters, and diaries. Still, a student's Fourth Amendment right to privacy is limited. The *T.L.O.* decision states, "The Fourth Amendment does not protect subjective expectations of privacy that are unreasonable or otherwise 'illegitimate.'"[2] In other words, students should not expect to have privacy regarding certain illegal activities, such as bringing weapons and drugs to school. The Fourth Amendment was not intended to protect evidence of criminal activity.

Balancing Act

The Court's recognition of students' privacy rights created a unique situation on school campuses. School campuses still had to be kept safe. In order to do this, school officials had to have some freedom to enforce the rules. This sometimes conflicted with students' rights. A compromise was necessary. As a result, the Court slightly limited students' privacy rights. It also reduced the requirements for school searches from "probable cause" to "reasonable suspicion."

The Court left the extent of the search to the judgment of a school official (usually the vice principal). A search can be as simple as looking in a student's purse or backpack. It may include a body search. This means the searcher would pat down the suspect through his or her clothing. In extremely serious situations, the school official may decide to order a strip search. This type of search is done by an official of the same gender as the accused. It requires the removal of clothing. The decision to do a strip search must be made very carefully. Parents and students consider this an extreme action. Lawsuits against the school are likely if all the rules are not followed.

Any search conducted by the school must be reasonable. The decision to search must be based on the suspected violation and what the searcher expects to find. For example, running in the hall or talking in class would not justify a search. A vice principal might decide to search the purse or pockets of a student thought to have violated the school's smoking rules. A student accused of theft or possession of drugs might have his or her locker searched and might be patted down. The student's age and gender must be considered in the search decision. For example, a sixteen-year-old girl would be searched differently than a sixteen-year-old boy. A sixteen-year-old girl would also be searched differently than a six-year-old girl.

Some have hoped that school searches could be stopped. Unfortunately, school violence and drug problems have been increasing across the nation. As a result, further limiting of students' privacy rights had to be considered.

A Worsening Situation

From the mid-1980s through the 1990s, school shootings captured the nation's headlines far too often. Although the violence occurred in only a small percent of United States schools, fear struck them all. Statistics concerning violence among teens indicate a serious problem that merits this fear. For example, a recent study by the U.S. Department of Justice and the National Association of School Psychologists indicates that on an average school day, about

➤ One hundred thousand children take guns to school.

➤ Fourteen thousand students are attacked on school property.

➤ One hundred sixty thousand students stay home out of fear of violence.[3]

Schools facing serious threats of violence must take preventative measures. In some schools, students must pass through metal detectors as they enter school grounds. Locker searches are common throughout the nation.

School authorities often must act quickly. They have little time to consider all the consequences of conducting a search. As a result, several cases have been filed, and decided, in lower courts. Some of these required further examination of constitutional rights. These cases were appealed to higher courts. Some were finally decided by the U.S. Supreme Court. One of these cases involved random drug testing of school athletes.

Drug Testing

At the beginning of the 1991 season, Oregon seventh-grader James Acton decided to try out for football. The Veronia School District had an established drug-testing policy. James and his parents, however, objected to random testing and did not sign the consent form. As a result, James was not allowed to play football. When asked why he refused to be tested, James answered, "Because I feel that they have no reason to think I was taking drugs."

The Actons believed that drug testing all athletes violated the students' right to privacy. They filed a suit against the Veronia School District. After being tried in the lower courts, the case was decided by the U.S. Supreme Court on June 26, 1995.

Before reaching their decision, the Justices considered several aspects of the case. These aspects included the fact that the school district had experienced a substantial increase in drug problems. The Justices also considered the impact of drug use on young people. In their view:

Arrest Rates for Violent Crimes, by Age
(with percent change, 1989–1994)

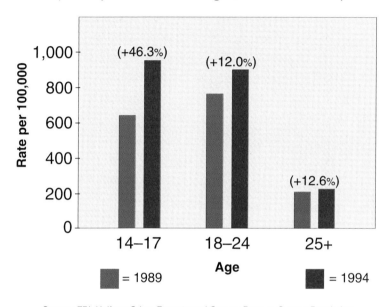

Source: *FBI, Uniform Crime Reports and Census Bureau, Current Population*

School years are the time when physical, psychological, and addictive effects of drugs are the most severe. . . . [T]he effects of a drug-infested school are visited not just upon the users, but upon the entire student body and faculty, as the educational process is disrupted.[4]

With this in mind, the Court ruled that the Veronia School District had a "compelling need" to control their drug problem.

The Justices also considered the fact that the Veronia athletes showered and dressed in open locker rooms without partitions (walls) for privacy.

••• 37 •••

In the Court's view, this situation lowered the expectation of privacy for the athletes. The Court also considered the method of collecting urine samples. Although the collections were monitored, students were allowed the same amount of privacy as they would expect during a routine visit to rest rooms. Thus, the Court ruled, "The invasion of privacy was not significant."[5] It found the Veronia policy "reasonable and hence constitutional."[6]

This decision applies only to the constitutional privacy rights involving drug testing for athletes. Many other aspects of student privacy rights are

*S*earching student lockers for drugs or weapons has created a debate over whether these searches violate students' privacy rights. In 1998, the Pennsylvania Supreme Court ruled that such a search was reasonable. Among other factors, they took into consideration the fact that lockers are school property and that students had been warned lockers would be searched.

being challenged in court by other students. For example, another case in a lower court dealt with locker searches, police assistance, and drug-sniffing dogs.

Locker Searches

A locker search on April 12, 1994, at Harborcreek High School in Philadelphia, Pennsylvania, resulted in a suit against the school. The school had received several reports indicating a drug problem on campus. Students had reported drug activity. Teachers had seen suspicious activities in the hallways. Concerned parents had called the school. And some students were known to be carrying large amounts of money.

Taking this information into consideration, the principal decided to conduct a locker search. Since there were two thousand lockers to search, the principal asked the local police to help. They assisted in the search with drug-sniffing dogs. During the search, marijuana, a pipe, a roach clip, and rolling papers were found in the locker of Vincent Cass. Eighteen-year-old Cass was suspended for ten days. Criminal drug charges were also filed against him.

In his defense, Cass's attorney claimed that the search violated Cass's Fourth Amendment right to privacy. He asked for suppression of the evidence. Harry Tischler, assistant general counsel with the school district, argued that the lockers belong to the school. He said, "The school district of Philadelphia has always had the position that it's our locker. We tell students you can't put your own lock on it, you can't share it . . . and you certainly can't put contraband [illegal objects] in it."[7]

The lower courts sided with Cass. The Pennsylvania Supreme Court, however, overturned the verdict in January 1998. It ruled that the school had a compelling (strong) interest in controlling drug use. The court also found that the search was reasonable. It considered several factors in making this decision:

➢ The lockers were school property.

➢ The lock combinations were kept in the school office.

➢ The lockers were frequently opened by school employees for repair.

➢ Students had been warned that locker searches would take place.

Therefore, the court ruled that students had only a "limited expectation of privacy" in their lockers.

The court further held that using drug-sniffing dogs does not violate the Fourth Amendment. Lawsuits concerning the use of drug-sniffing dogs and metal detectors have had different outcomes in other states. Such searches are allowed in some states and not in others.

Concern for Loss of Rights

The Pennsylvania Supreme Court decision was not unanimous. Five justices agreed while one dissented (disagreed). Justice Stephen Zappala wrote the dissenting opinion. He argued that because *police officers* conducted the locker search without *probable cause*, Cass's Fourth Amendment privacy rights were violated. He further contended that students do have a legitimate expectation of privacy in a school locker.[8]

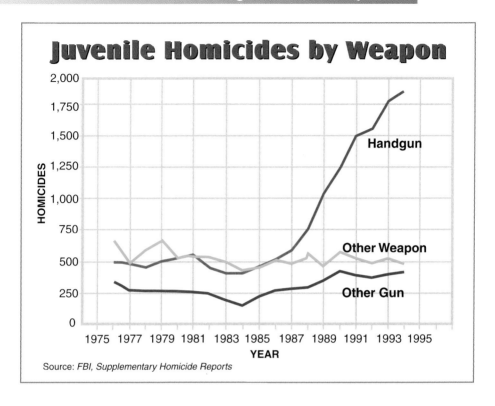

Juvenile Homicides by Weapon

HOMICIDES

2,000
1,750
1,500
1,250
1,000
750
500
250
0

Handgun

Other Weapon

Other Gun

1975 1977 1979 1981 1983 1985 1987 1989 1991 1993 1995
YEAR

Source: *FBI, Supplementary Homicide Reports*

Justice Zappala is not alone in his concern for the loss of students' privacy rights. Larry Frankel, executive director of the American Civil Liberties Union of Pennsylvania, expressed his concern. He said, "Schools have become places where children give up their rights almost completely."[9]

Tug-of-War

These state supreme court decisions helped define students' privacy rights. They also set some school search guidelines. Violation of students' privacy rights during drug testing and locker searches is a valid concern. The threat to safety brought by drugs and violence is also serious. These two concerns can come into conflict. Some people have strong feelings on both sides of the issue. School

*A*bout one hundred thousand students now bring guns to school. This has led to an increase in school violence and school shootings.

authorities are caught in a tug-of-war between those who fight for privacy rights and those who fight for safe school campuses.

The conflict between rights and safety is not new. Supreme Court Justice Thurgood Marshall expressed his concern for the loss of rights in a 1989 dissenting opinion for *Skinner* v. *Railway Labor Executive Association*. The issue before the Court concerned safety and the drug testing of railroad workers. Warning against sacrificing fundamental constitutional freedoms during a time of crisis, he wrote:

> Precisely because the need for action against the drug scourge is manifest, the need for vigilance against unconstitutional excess is great. History teaches that grave threats to liberty often come in times of urgency, when constitutional rights seem too extravagant to endure.[10]

In other words, Justice Marshall warned that once rights are lost, they are very hard to regain.

Chapter 5

Knowing Your Rights

There are many areas involving privacy rights for students. Some of these are not likely to attract media attention or become court cases. Abuse of these rights, however, may greatly affect a student's future. Students must know their rights so that they can defend themselves against violations and protect their privacy. For example, they should be aware of the Family Educational Rights and Privacy Act.

Education Records

Congress passed the Family Educational Rights and Privacy Act (FERPA) in 1974. FERPA makes educational records private. Educational records contain the student's grade history and grade point average, SAT/GRE test scores, family income, parents' names, and medical information. They may also include teachers' notes about the student's behavior or learning problems. A student's educational record begins when he or she first enters school. It is kept forever. The parents hold their child's FERPA rights

*T*he Family Educational Rights and Privacy Act (FERPA) makes educational records private. The act covers records such as a student's grade history, standardized test scores, and medical information.

until the child becomes an "eligible student." This happens when the child reaches eighteen years of age or enters college. At that time, the rights pass from the parents to the child. The parents no longer have access to the child's educational records.

Rights concerning educational records include:

➤ The right to review one's educational records.

➤ The right to request correction of inaccurate or misleading information.

➤ The right to have personal information excluded from school directories.

➤ The right to file a complaint with the U.S. Department of Education if the school violates FERPA.

➤ Personally identifiable information contained in the record cannot be released to anyone outside the school without written consent from the parent or student.[1]

Schools can release information for research. They can also provide statistics that are not personally identifiable. For example, a statement such as "Jane Smith made an *A* in history" would be personally identifiable. This could not be released. A statement such as "Fifteen girls made *A*s in history" could be released. Although information from all the girls' records was used to compile the information, none of the girls can be identified by this information. It is not personally identifiable.

FERPA allows only certain people access to educational records. These include the parents or eligible students and school officials with "legitimate educational interest" in the information. A school official has a legitimate educational interest if he or she needs information to help the student in some way.[2] This might be understanding a student's learning disability. It could also be the need to control a behavior problem.

Keeping educational records private may not seem important. In the computer age, however, vast amounts of information can be stored and searched. No one knows how one piece of information may be linked to another. And no one knows how the information might used. As a result, all privacy rights need to be protected.

Court Records

In the past, young lawbreakers had a right to privacy. Juvenile courts were closed. This barred the public, including reporters, from the courtroom. When the media reported a crime committed by a juvenile, the child's face was not shown. Names of juveniles were withheld. For further privacy protection, all juvenile criminal records were closed. No one could view the records without authority to do so. Upon reaching eighteen, the offender could petition the court to have his or her records destroyed. This privacy right was written into the juvenile code of most states. It was based on the idea that a person should not pay for youthful mistakes throughout his or her life. Society expected that young offenders would learn from their mistakes and become law-abiding adults.

In recent years, however, juvenile crime has increased. It has also become more violent. In tracking juvenile delinquents, researchers have found that many of them continue to commit crimes after they reach age eighteen. In view of this trend, by 1996 at least forty-eight states had passed laws ending the juvenile privacy privilege. This opened juvenile court records.[3] Many people have supported this move. They believe that releasing the information helps protect society from repeat offenders.[4] Whether committed by a youth or adult, crime involves many people. These include the criminal, the victims, potential victims, and the families of each of these people.

Medical Care

Health problems, however, are a private matter (except in cases of contagious disease). Medical records of the young and old are protected and private. Parents are the guardians of their children's health-care privacy rights. They have a right to be informed of their child's medical condition. They make the decisions and pay the bills. Except in an emergency, they must consent to the child's medical treatment.

Sometimes an older child may wish to seek medical advice without the parents' knowledge. This may bring the parental guardianship and the child's interest into conflict.

Federal and state lawmakers recognize the value of parental involvement in children's health care. In recent years, however, they have realized that some young people need health care privacy. Otherwise, these teens may not seek medical advice or treatment for certain health concerns. These areas include sexuality and mental health. As a result, these teens may not get professional advice about contraception (birth control) or safe sex. They may delay getting treatment for sexually transmitted diseases, such as herpes or gonorrhea. They may avoid treatment for drug abuse. Pregnant teens may not get the advice they need. Serious health problems can develop in all these areas. Some are life-threatening. Lawmakers have seen the need to change health-care privacy laws. They have taken steps to give teenagers privacy in some areas of health care.[5]

Abortion and contraception for minors, however, are extremely controversial issues. People with liberal political beliefs tend to support more privacy for minors. Those with a conservative viewpoint want parents to have control. Therefore, state laws regarding these issues are subject to change as new legislators take office. Legislators work to pass laws that reflect their political viewpoint and the views of the people they represent.

A 1997 analysis of state laws found that minors had the right to privacy in seeking:

- ➤ contraceptive services in twenty-three states and the District of Columbia

- ➤ prenatal care and delivery services in twenty-seven states and the District of Columbia

- ➤ treatment for sexually transmitted disease in forty-nine states and the District of Columbia

- ➤ confidential counseling and medical care for drug and/or alcohol abuse in forty-five states and the District of Columbia

- ➤ mental health services in twenty-one states and the District of Columbia[6]

At that time, no state had an ironclad requirement for parental involvement in obtaining any of these medical services. In addition, married minors are considered adults and can make their own medical decisions. They can also make decisions concerning their children.

Abortion is a different matter. In 1997, only two states had laws that allowed a minor to obtain an abortion on her own.[7] Twenty-nine states required the involvement of at least one parent in a minor's abortion decision.[8]

By 1998 the statistics had changed. Thirty-nine states required parental consent or notification before a minor could obtain an abortion.[9] Most state laws include a judicial bypass. This means that a judge may give consent for an abortion if contacting the parents is not desirable.

*W*hen a baby is adopted, his or her records are sealed to keep the identity of the birth mother secret. However, Congress is considering the creation of a national adoption registry to make it easier for birth parents and adopted children to find each other.

Adoption Records

Most states do not require parental consent for a minor to place her child up for adoption.[10] In the past, many adoption agencies kept the mother's identity secret. In addition, a law passed in 1973 sealed all adoption records.[11] This meant that no one outside the agency could see these records. As a result, when a child was adopted, a new birth certificate was created listing the adoptive parents. The old one was sealed along with other records of the adoption.

In recent years, however, some adoption records have been opened by court order. This happens when health information about the birth parents could aid in a child's medical treatment. For example, a child needing a bone marrow transplant might find a donor. Once certain records were opened, other people wanted to find birth parents.

Today many adopted children demand information that will help them find their birth parents. As a result, Congress is considering the possibility of creating a national adoption registry.[12] This would make it easier for birth parents and adopted children to find each other. Some people think it would be unfair to birth mothers who wish to remain unidentified. Others think this information is the child's right.

Today's teen mother might find herself on both sides of this issue. She could be seeking privacy in giving up her own child for adoption. At the same time, she could be an adoptee longing to find her birth parents.

A crack in the privacy shield between adopted child and birth parent already exists. A vast amount of family history information is stored in computer databases and on the Internet.

Chapter 6

Privacy in Cyberspace

Two recent changes in particular have increased the risk of privacy invasion for young people. The first change is related to the booming popularity of the Internet. In 1998, about 10 million minors were using the Internet in the United States. More than four times that number (42 million) are expected to be online by 2002.[1]

The second change has to do with buying power. In 1998, a polling firm called Teenage Research Unlimited did a survey. They asked teens about their spending habits. They found that the average teen spends about three hundred dollars of his or her own money each month.[2] Overall, this adds up to an impressive sum. The buying power of America's youth also includes the billions of dollars their parents spend on them. These items include brand-name clothing, computer games, electronic toys, and sporting goods. In 1997, teenagers and children influenced or made purchases that added a $47 billion boost to the U.S. economy.[3]

This massive amount of buying power has not

escaped the notice of big companies. They have also noticed young people's interest in the Internet. As a result, their marketing experts have focused on young people who surf the Net.

Commercial Web Pages

Companies that target young people create colorful Web sites. They offer games, contests, and prizes. Many sites also offer opportunities to interact with popular cartoon characters or celebrities. The sites attract children and teens like magnets.

The Web sites often contain registration forms. The forms must be completed before a visitor can take part in the activities. These forms provide useful information for the company. The Federal Trade Commission conducted a survey of fourteen hundred Web sites in March 1998. The survey revealed that 90 percent of the most popular children's sites asked for information that would identify the child.[4] This is called personally identifiable information. It includes name, address, and phone number.

Many companies also track Net surfers from site to site. They do this by planting software codes called "cookies" on each visitor's hard drive. Some cookies only allow the site to recognize returning guests or registered numbers. Other cookies, however, can record other sites the surfer visits on the Internet. When the surfer returns to the original site, the collected information is delivered to the company's database. In this way, companies gain detailed information about the surfer's interests.

The companies can sort the people listed in their databases according to interest and create mailing lists. These mailing lists are valuable. Some companies sell these lists to other companies. The lists allow a company to target likely buyers. They can advertise to the people who are most likely to buy their products. In this way, they can get the most from their marketing dollar. This type of advertising is often sent by e-mail.

The Federal Trade Commission (FTC) considers the use of information collected without the person's knowledge an invasion of privacy. They also consider targeting children in this manner an unfair trade practice. The U.S. government took steps to address the matter in 1998.

Children's Online Privacy Protection Act of 1998

On October 21, 1998, Congress passed the Children's Online Privacy Protection Act. This act is designed to regulate marketing practices on the Internet. As a result of this act, Web sites are now required to obtain parental consent before gathering information about children who are twelve and under. In addition, parents must be able to view the information collected from the child. They may also limit the use of that information.[5]

This act was the first step toward privacy protection on the Internet. Many people feel that the act should have protected all Internet users.[6] They want Congress to pass additional legislation.

Lawmakers hoped that further regulation of company Web sites would not be necessary. They wanted the companies to regulate themselves. The government studied Web site practices before and after the act was passed. A few months before it was enacted, they found that 14 percent of sites posted a privacy notice. These notices alert visitors that the

*F*requent-shopper cards, such as this one for the Safeway Club, offer shoppers discounts on their purchases. However, since some frequent-shopper cards can track what people buy, some people consider them a threat to privacy.

site gathers information. They also explain how the information will be used. The visitor can then decide whether to fill out the registration form. Six months after passage of the act, the number of Web sites with privacy notices rose to 66 percent. Some feel this proves that the industry will regulate itself. Others still think more government regulation is needed.[7]

Danger on the Web

Law enforcement agencies worry about other dangers that lurk on the Internet. For example, information on personal Web sites can be viewed by anyone. Some viewers may have criminal intent. In addition, criminals may set up their own Web sites to collect information. Some criminals may find their victims this way.

Pedophiles and child molesters prey on children. These criminals have been known to frequent on-line bulletin boards and chat rooms. They work to gain a child's confidence while exchanging friendly messages. On the computer in his or her own room, the child feels safe. A child who gives a stranger too much personal information, however, can become a victim. Often, the criminal's goal is to lure the child into meeting in person.[8] Sometimes the child becomes a victim of a violent crime. This is the worst kind of privacy invasion. It is the worst abuse of information. Too often it results in injury or death.

Young people also face a privacy threat on their own Web pages. Great care should be taken in what is displayed on a Web page. Personal information may lead a criminal to the owner of the page or to someone in his or her family. Information such as name, address, phone number, age, and school should not appear on a Web page.

Safety Rules in Cyberspace

Protecting privacy on the Internet includes keeping personal information secret. It also includes protection from disturbing e-mail. Disturbing messages might threaten and harass. They may be obscene or pornographic.

These easy-to-follow rules will provide safety and protect the privacy of young Net surfers:

> ➤ Use a "handle" (false name) when taking part in a chat room or bulletin board discussion.

➤ Never give identifying information—actual name, address, school name, or telephone number—in a chat room or bulletin board.

➤ Beware! An e-mail pen pal may lie.
A thirty-five-year-old criminal may pretend to be a friendly twelve-year-old girl.

➤ Never agree to a face-to-face meeting with anyone you meet on the Internet.

➤ Tell your parents at once if you find disturbing material on the Internet, or if someone asks you to meet in person.

➤ Do not respond to disturbing e-mail.[9]

Knowledgeable young people are their own first line of defense against privacy invasion and criminal activity on the Internet.

Other Threats

As technology advances, people of all ages are losing privacy. In fact, a small amount of information is collected every time someone dials an 800 or 900 telephone number. Other information is collected from warranty cards, contest entry forms, and magazine subscriptions. Additional information is gathered by book and record clubs. If you use a grocery store card, the store is tracking your purchases. These bits of information reveal a little about a person.

None of these methods alone poses a great threat to privacy. The major threat develops over time. Companies and government agencies assign numbers to customers and citizens. This includes driver's licenses, credit cards, Social Security numbers, and medical record numbers. Much of a person's life is recorded in files under these numbers. Additional information resides in birth, marriage, voter registration, and property records. As long as the contents of these files remain separate, written on paper, and filed in manila envelopes where only authorized personnel can access them, they pose little threat to privacy.

These public and private files contain some information in common. For example, most of these records contain a person's Social Security number. Other common information in each file includes name, address, and date of birth. A person might use different names and change addresses. The Social Security number and birth date, however, remain the same. In the digital age, many of these records are being stored in large computer databases. A computer search can gather information from several of these sources. In this way, the details of a person's life can be gathered into one place. This could have advantages for everyone. It could also have disadvantages. It could prove to be a disaster.

A computer-savvy snooper could type in a name, hit the Enter key, and trigger a search of many databases. In fact, the snooper could obtain information on any person he or she chooses.[10] Along with the person's name, address, and phone number, such a search might reveal past addresses, buying habits, and schools attended. It might also reveal employment history, health conditions, and disease history. Other information might include marital status, the names of the person's spouse, children, friends, and family members. A snooper might find out about a person's political activity, arrests, or convictions.

In a 1997 speech, Secretary of Health and Human Services Donna Shalala stated,

> Our most cherished and personal information . . . flow[s] freely through computers open to virtually everyone. . . . [T]he computer revolution means that our deepest and darkest secrets no longer exist in one place and can no longer be protected by simply locking up the office doors each night.[11]

As technology advances, information gatherers can pry further into our private lives. This growing threat reaches into every aspect of an individual's life, from birth to beyond death. Despite the threat, young people can still benefit from the vast amount of information available on the Internet. There are many benefits to the computer age. These benefits and conveniences, however, make privacy very hard to protect.

Chapter 1. How Privacy Became an Issue

1. *New Jersey* v. *T.L.O.*, 469 U.S. 325 (1985).

2. Ibid.

3. Randy M. Page and Jon Hammermeister, "Weapon-carrying and Youth Violence," *Adolescence*, vol. 32, September 22, 1997, pp. 505–509.

4. U.S. Department of Education, "1999 Annual Report on School Safety," Office of Elementary and Secondary Education, p. 5.

5. *New Jersey* v. *T.L.O.*

Chapter 2. The Reasons for Privacy

1. *Olmstead* v. *United States*, 277 U.S. 438, 478 (1928).

2. "The Quartering Act, March 24, 1765," *Lexrex*, <http://www.lexrex.com/enlightened/laws/quartering.htm> (February 8, 1999).

3. Arthur M. Schlesinger, Jr., *The Almanac of American History* (New York: Barnes & Noble Books, 1993), p. 114.

4. Quoted in Roger Rosenblatt, "The Bill of Rights: The First of the 10 Amendments Launches Us on a Journey of Self-discovery," *Life*, October 15, 1991, p. 9.

5. Ibid.

6. Constitution of the United States, Third Amendment, Ratified December 15, 1791.

7. James Otis, "In Opposition to Writs of Assistance," February 1761, <http://www.nationalcenter.inter.net/OppositiontoWrits.html> (February 16, 1999).

8. Constitution of the United States, Fourth Amendment, Ratified December 15, 1791.

9. *Miranda* v. *Arizona*, 384 U.S. 435 (1966).

10. "Miranda Rights," <http://www.duidefense.com/arrest/miranda.htm> (February 9, 1999).

Chapter 3. Student Rights Go to Court

1. *Tinker* v. *Des Moines Independent School District*, 393 U.S. 503 (1969).

2. *Goss* v. *Lopez*, 419 U.S. 565 (1975).

3. Ibid.

4. Ellen Alderman and Caroline Kennedy, *The Right to Privacy* (New York: Alfred A. Knopf, 1995), p. 37.

5. Ibid., pp. 38–39.

6. Ibid., p. 39.

7. *New Jersey* v. *T.L.O.*, 469 U.S. 325, (1985).

8. Ibid.

Chapter 4. Resolving the Unanswered Questions

1. *New Jersey* v. *T.L.O.*, 469 U.S. 325, (1985).

2. Ibid.

3. "Preventing and Coping with School Violence: A Resource Manual for Washington School Employees," July 1995, <http://www.wa.nea.org/PUBLICAT/Legal/PRVNTSV2.HTM#anchor247024> (June 16, 2000).

4. *Veronia School District* v. *Wayne Acton*, 515 U.S. 646 (1995).

5. Ibid.

6. Ibid.

7. Richard Jones and Connie Langland, "High Court Gives Schools Right to Search Lockers," *Philadelphia Inquirer*, January 9, 1998, p. B2.

8. *Commonwealth of Pennsylvania* v. *Cass*, 551 Pa. 25 (1998).

9. Jones and Langland, p. B2.

10. Quoted in William F. Woo, "Balancing Safety and Our Liberty," *St. Louis Post-Dispatch*, January 9, 1994, p. B1.

Chapter 5. Knowing Your Rights

1. Family Educational Rights and Privacy Act (FERPA), <http://www.lrp.com/ed/freelib/free_regs/bc3499.htm> (November 8, 1999).

2. Wake Forest University, "Family Educational Rights & Privacy Act," The Lake Forest Information Network (WIN), <http://www.wfu.edu/parents/academic-policies.html#ferpa> (November 8, 1999).

3. "Emerging Juvenile Offender Laws Tougher on Teens," *All Things Considered* (National Public Radio), August 8, 1996.

4. Judith VandeWater, "Violent Crime Brings Changing View of Juvenile Codes: Some Officials Favor Opening Up of Information of Young Offenders," *St. Louis Post-Dispatch*, January 3, 1995, p. 1.

5. Pat Donovan, "Special Analysis: Teens' Ability to Consent to Reproductive Health Care Commonly Recognized at State Level," *Contemporary Women's Issues Database*, vol. 8, September 1, 1997, p. 3ff.

6. Ibid.

7. Ibid.

8. Ibid.

9. "Restrictions on Minors' Access to Abortion," *NARAL Factsheets*, National Abortion and Reproductive Rights Action League Foundation, December 1998, <http://www.naral.org/publications/facts/minor.html> (April 29, 1999).

10. Patricia Donovan, "Our Daughters' Decisions—The Conflict in State Law on Abortion & Other Issues (part 5 of 6)," *Contemporary Women's Issues Database*, January 1, 1992, pp. 23–28.

11. Christopher Lee, "Bill Pits Adoptees' Wishes, Parents' Privacy Hopes: Panel Weighs Emotional Factors of Records Issue," *The Dallas Morning News*, March 7, 1999, p. 45A.

12. Anick Jesdanun, "Adoptees Speak on National Registry," *AP Online*, June 12, 1998, Electronic Library, (May 7, 1999).

Chapter 6. Privacy in Cyberspace

1. "Fact Sheet No. 21: Children in Cyberspace," *Privacy Rights Clearinghouse*, December 29, 1998, <http://www.privacyrights.org/fs/children.htm> (January 25, 1999).

2. Anne Veigle, "Creating Generation $$$; Products Pitched to Youngsters With Money to Burn," *The Washington Times*, May 11, 1999, p E1.

3. Ibid.

4. Mary Mosquera, "Net Privacy Bill for Kids Expected to Pass," *TechWeb Internet*, September 23, 1998, <http://techsearch.techweb.com/internet/story/TWB19980923S0011> (January 7, 1999).

5. Jeff Chester, "Congress Passes First Legislation on Internet Privacy and Children," *Center for Media Education Press Release*, October 21, 1998, <http://epn.org/cme/pr102198.html> (May 3, 1999).

6. Ibid.

7. Ted Bridis, "Study Finds Web Site Privacy Warnings Improve," *The Arizona Republic*, May 13, 1999, p. D5.

8. Lawrence J. Magid, "Child Safety on the Information Highway," *National Center for Missing and Exploited Children*, 1994, <http://www.reseau-medias.ca/eng/med/home/resource/childsaf.htm> (May 3, 1999).

9. Ibid.

10. Leslie Miller, "Prying Eyes: No Solitude in Cyberspace," *USA Today*, June 9, 1997, p. D1.

11. Robert A. Rosenblatt, "Shalala Calls for New Health Privacy Laws; Rights: Computers and Insurance Are Altering Doctor-Patient Relationship, HHS Chief Says. Video Rental Records are More Protected than Medical Files," *Los Angeles Times*, August 1, 1997, p. A20.

Books:

Day, Nancy. *Violence in Schools: Learning in Fear.* Springfield, N.J.: Enslow Publishers, Inc., 1996.

Dolan, Edward F. *Your Privacy: Protecting It in a Nosy World.* New York: Cobblehill Books, 1995.

Faber, Doris, and Harold Faber. *We the People: The Story of the Constitution Since 1787.* New York: Scribners, 1987.

Krull, Kathleen. *A Kid's Guide to America's Bill of Rights: Curfews, Censorship, and the 100-pound Giant.* New York: Avon Books, 1999.

Meltzer, Milton. *The Bill of Rights: How We Got It and What It Means.* New York: Thomas Y. Crowell, 1990.

Newton, David E. *Drug Testing: An Issue for School, Sports, and Work.* Springfield N.J.: Enslow Publishers, Inc., 1999.

Stein, Richard Conrad. *The Bill of Rights.* Danbury, Conn.: Children's Press, 1994.

Internet Sites:

Magid, Lawrence J. *Child Safety on the Information Highway.* National Center for Missing and Exploited Children.
<http://www.ncmec.org>
See Education & Resources, Library of Resources, Child Safety Information

Privacy Rights Clearinghouse.
<http://www.privacyrights.org>